The Past and This

Sinchan Chakraborty

Ukiyoto Publishing

All global publishing rights are held by

Ukiyoto Publishing

Published in 2024

Content Copyright © Sinchan Chakraborty

ISBN 9789361728273

*All rights reserved.
No part of this publication may be reproduced,
transmitted, or stored in a retrieval system, in any form
by any means, electronic, mechanical, photocopying,
recording or otherwise, without the prior permission of
the publisher.*

The moral rights of the authors have been asserted.

*This is a work of fiction. Names, characters, businesses,
places, events, locales, and incidents are either the
products of the author's imagination or used in a fictitious
manner. Any resemblance to actual persons, living or
dead, or actual events is purely coincidental.*

*This book is sold subject to the condition that it shall not by
way of trade or otherwise, be lent, resold, hired out or
otherwise circulated, without the publisher's prior
consent, in any form of binding or cover other than that in
which it is published.*

www.ukiyoto.com

Acknowledgement

I'd like to use this page to let my readers know that the entire set of shared words that they've just read has a touch of my beloved who never knew that HE is the one.
I want to thank my Mother and my elder Sister who believed in me and still does, at every point of moment I take a decision and stand by me.

Contents

The Story of the Past	1
My thought's My frenemy	5
Questions	9
It Is You	13
The Hope's Palace	19
On The Bedside wall	21

About the Author   *26*

The Story of the Past

It's 5 AM. The soul's sitting alone, my mind feeling so bright,
Is it the early morning or the middle of the night?
The wind still howls the winter tune;
and trees are dancing in the dale,
I yearn for sun and summer's warmth…
but all I get is cold and hail.
Cold and hail, it's the atmospheric alarm,
While my mind shivers to calm!
A comeback, is it what this is about?
The mind that once gave up
The heart that cried
Will that both work for the soul to count?

Imagine how things could be
Callous words are dead
And life dwells there instead
Acceptance is joy
Rejection is pain
You don't have to feel negative feelings ever again
Things can happen and might go wrong,
Fear and hate are my greatest enemies
Running away and fighting back

The Past and This

But there is one place I can go
The land of memories!
Witty comebacks, classy moves
Everyone loves you just the way you are!
Imagine it all
It could be
Except it isn't
A memory, an insult, a kiss
A memory,
That moment might fade away
But the scar gets worse
Irrespective of a night or a day
An insult,
Those words meant pain
Those emotions were hurt
The moment might be gone
but the thought of the same will come back again.
A kiss,
Just a kiss, a one-time thing to try
Nothing's attached but
Butterflies… with a beat being skipped
there's nothing to ask but the heart wants to fly

Haunted,
Although when others say "Boo!" to him,
He's prepared,
Not scared

Worries and fears are no longer a worry,
It's normal,
For him,
He climbed back into his world,
Inch by inch, mostly into the darkness,
Until he was no longer afraid of enjoying the light,
Which is now

I now know him, a new self who was born
While the time's take a toll
My mind gathers those pieces, once torn

I'm standing at the window, waiting for
The cloud's half-hunter to unclip the moon,
A pebble yowl, uniquely nondescript,
So, this last week's equation stays unsolved
Inside the jotter, a sum of many parts.
The tune you play
Let's take a walk by the bay
I love the old me who cried
But the new me won't repeat what he tried
You found me though and play a small guitar,
Somewhere behind me. I envisage you
Cross-legged at the centre of my room.
Since you have stripped off, I resolve to start
The correlation, shapes up things to come,
To pull the wishbone, shed some light on you.

The Past and This

To ask for a day
To make it up to him
The old one grieved over the past
The new me laughs at what he did last

You tell me that your firebrand days have waned;
The night grows hotter. High time you explained
Maybe my ex never mansplained
But the love we had did give me a reason
To relive again without letting it go in vain.

My thought's My frenemy

A friend, a mind speaker, that's my frenemy;

Causing a charm with a hint of a fanity,

Overthinking is my enemy.

It leads me to complete insanity.

I made peace with my overthinking

And suddenly forgot how to do it

A bit by a bit, at last it gave its last hit.

Noticeable moments, where overthinking has no room,

Four or five, aren't all a happy married bride and groom.

Where a flicker of unexplainable joy finds you at peace,

For a moment you're not worried about anything, which too shall cease.

Start a new day,

6   The Past and This

Know precisely what to say.
Prove your peers,
That you have got, what it takes.
Indulge in things,
That gives you wings.
Unnecessary doubts, don't let that bother
Maintain your mind to train for the newest things.

The monster behind my downfall,
I'm wondering if I could break free and stand tall!
The side they never talk about
The moment when I skipped death was proud.
But fear clouds my judgment;
Disappointment builds up and the storm starts redying.
Caught in a cyclone, of my own cynical thinking.
Overthinking thinks the usual smoking does,
I know it harms my peace, degrades my calm
But the 2am thoughts
Do kick my butt, still onto my "left out" palm.

I lost my breath

With a deep exhaled sigh,

Then I remind myself

Of what it's like to overdose the drug's high.

Tell me! Tell me!

Give me a fact, a worthy reason;

What makes love such an ache and pain

When all it does is just to shower like the season's first rain.

A stormy night

I'll hold my grip tight

Your love ached my heart

But calmed my mind when we did part.

Overthinking sucks,

Smoking kills,

Both the causes are injurious to our race

For we can't undo a fact,

"Can we ever check for a reality, going for confrontation to the face?"

The Past and This

Never mind, it's all in my head!
At the end I'll just lie on my bed!
When the night falls down,
The powdered happiness intake with frown
Never cry for help, nobody shows up.
Until it's now
And that's when people say!
He was a good guy though;
Who ended his life, the question is 'HOW!'

QUESTIONS

Depression on my Left,
Loneliness on my right,
Hold on to your breath,
The heart now needs to get a grip, Tight.
No sound from the crowd!
No cries to be heard!
There is no feeling that has changed...

Is there a way to call off this fight?

- Do they blame the present?
- I threw mud in the past!
The time flows by
I can't cope, my walk isn't that fast.
Admire the happiness that doesn't stay for long
Why did you call me in?
Is crying the only thing, where did I go wrong?

The Past and This

Is looking for a reason, a crime to commit?

Was asking for some space, a disgusting pukish vomit?

Do my smiles answer for me, even if it's fake?

Were my screams never heard, just because it wasn't my take?

I wish life was better than the words that they share,

I wish they spoke to me instead of their unconcerned show of CARE.

I feel like drowning in depression

Why is everything turning into a lesson?

Life is hard. With each second now it's stressing,

Hello People! Can you tell me, what did I do wrong?

Can you tell me why I do not own a blessing?

Can you please tell me why am I not Strong?

Tears are for losers

Wiped them in fear

Injuries don't hurt

Plucked the wound using tweezers

I am trying! I am trying
That is all I do
I never asked to be a part
I never counted myself in your few

Never wanted myself included
You chose me
Got me out as soon as my part was done
Don't get me in your plans
Never really asked for a seat
But the moment I was made to feel at home
Someone shook me to reality!
"Get out, you aren't required!"

I'm trying to live and love without feeling distressed
I'm trying hard to keep my feelings unexpressed
Can you at least have mercy on me
And leave me by myself to a count of three
One, take away this depressing loneliness
Two, I am not alone, but I still am

The Past and This

Three, With family and friends

still, I am stuck in a traffic jam

The traffic of thoughts curdled with the sadness behind

Can you provide me a day to let him look for me and find

Find what I have staged this long

Find that I have curtained myself and I didn't do anything wrong

Bipolar depression pulls me back

It's not me who lets myself go off the track

I am happy a day before the next day I'm sad

It is the condition that has made me go this bad

I need time, I will be fine

The guy who smiles every time will bring back his shine

IT IS YOU

Bring me your pain, love.

The world's making me go insane

Spread it out like fine rugs,silk sashes,

Damn! Why do I not get high on drugs?

warm eggs, cinnamon

and cloves in burlap sacks.

Show me how you got that taste

Show me how will you paint me

On the walls if I was a thing to paste.

At the touch of you,

No-one knew

I hate being touched

But I tendered when you do

The Past and This

As if you were an archer

with your swift hand at the bow,

getting my body close to yours, just at a go!

The arrows of delight shot through my body

The sheer eye look made my throat go dry

Decoded the name which will make me smile

I wasn't forced because you didn't try.

I hushed to turn the lights off

Touching you I catch the midnight

as moon fires set in my throat,

I glanced outside towards the moonlight

I love you, flesh into blossom

I made you mine

and took you to a place where nothing is fine.

Last night I slept, and when I woke your kiss

Still floated on my lips. For we had strayed

Together in my dream, through some dim glade,

Where the shy moonbeams scarce dared light our bliss.

You came to the side of the bed

and sat staring at me.

Then you kissed me, I felt

hot wax on my forehead.

I wanted it to leave a mark:

That's how I knew I loved you.

And that's how I knew

It's you; It's you: its nobody but is you

The Past and This

In your arms you hold me tight,

Never letting go through the night.

All my dreams are peaceful because of you,

Holding me in your arms like you do.

I like how that feels

To say your name as if it brings down some chills

To hold you close, to have you near

To have my breath against your ear

You squeeze me tight

I scratch my nails on you back as if it's a FIGHT

Whispering the words I long to say

Being able to show you my passion in that special way,

Just the way you caress my hair, touch my palm and put it on your chest

Like in the morning you drop me off; to my stop,

he never bids me goodbye for he says

"I'll be here until u return and I get u some rest"

The loving, caressing, kissing would feel so right

Expressing our love right through the night

Would care for me all day

Would take me out for dates

and at times out for a walk by the bay.

Its night! I woke up gasping for some air

It's a nightmare, but I'm scared to call it fair

that hug calms me down

Words being whispered about the dream to be wrong

The Past and This

You came to the side of the bed

and sat staring at me.

Then you kissed me, I felt

The love in your eyes

It's just for a moment, I thought

When you too said.

This is why I know I love you

My heart skipped a bit

When you too said

Love me like I do,

For! It's you;

its nobody but is you,

It has always been you.

The Hope's Palace

A moment of silence acquired the room,

Which once echoed with laughter, gossip and noise

Now there's no one to say who is that, from a "where" to a "whom"

A rupee or a coin, a price to a poise.

I slammed the door shut

Broke the Palace of hope

The former cheated but, still termed the latter to be a slut

Untied the happiness which once they both tied with a love bond named rope!

Truth be told, that wasn't love but anything;

It was just a two minute's affection that evaporated and shattered everything.

I'm like a lock to which you were the key,

The Past and This

That moment of silence now feels suffocating and not any air to breathe in free.

A moment of silence acquired the room!

Now we are strangers

No words that we used to term

each other as a "my who to your whom"

Now we're strangers!

Crossing our paths would be the last thing

from that "where" we began to that end of my empty bedroom

On The Bedside Wall

When everything goes wrong

Every day isn't the same

as a ding for a dong.

for that wants to tame

when nothing goes right;

And everything around you hovers to fight.

And you wonder why this morning you woke!

Everything you made is now shattered and broke

The wind around you seem to scream;

And no one seems to wonder,

what those words actually mean.

Everything that normally comforts you is gone,

And you find your soul alone living a sad pity song.

The Past and This

Life is like a game

Come on KID roll the dice

Either turns a stone

Or breaks that bit of ice

All you did is play around

And now your name is for the "lost and found"

Now you did pick a card

That reads 'jack of all trades, master of none'

for at the game's end, nothing really is done

You move two spaces ahead

You did something right

But nothing matters

Something will happen later

Bad or worse, which you must fight

When you change, the game too changes

The game changes along you my friend

Got too deep into dying in hell

You won't be able to get out;

For you'll be wrapped in chains,

And nobody will be able to tell!

Until the tears roll down,

Like the cloud showers while it rains.

Suffering? Suffering u say? That is a mandate.

It increases exponentially.

At my age,

It isn't a number but some rate.

My heart and mind are

Full of suppurating burns

And I suffer every moment

The Past and This

As this life takes unexpected turns.

I had a sleepless night.

Making plans ahead

But the day comes without news

That turns everything upside down

Without a call for a decision

My peace asks me to stay in bed

Stay here, stay for a while

Within my four walls

I feel safe and sound

No worse to fight

No words to be shared

I don't have it in me anymore

That used to make me the person who was right!

That used to make me the person who was happy

And didn't care if he'd be asked to fight.

About the Author

Sinchan Chakraborty

A literature major's soul in an Engineer's body. A poet, a fun-loving guy, and a gentleman with a calm and composed self that controls his mind to work. Sinchan Chakraborty- who dabbles with quirky replies and a commendable work ethic. A poet who knows what his words are and he is the one who knows how to work his way out of it.

www.ingramcontent.com/pod-product-compliance
Lightning Source LLC
LaVergne TN
LVHW041643070526
838199LV00053B/3528